How To Handle Risk:

Mastering the Art of Risk and Navigating Uncertainties with Confidence

WENDY A. JOHNSON

Introduction To Risk Management

Handling risk is an essential skill that impacts individuals, businesses, and societies at large. As life is inherently unpredictable, the ability to recognize, assess, and manage risk becomes paramount in achieving success and minimizing negative consequences. From financial investments and business ventures to personal decisions and everyday activities, risk is an ever-present factor that demands thoughtful consideration and preparation.

In this context, a comprehensive understanding of risk management principles empowers individuals and organizations to make informed choices and effectively navigate through uncertainties. By adopting a proactive approach, acknowledging potential threats, and implementing appropriate measures, one can reduce the likelihood of adverse outcomes and seize opportunities that arise amidst challenges.

This topic delves into the fundamental concepts of risk management, exploring various methodologies, tools, and strategies to confront uncertainties head-on. It emphasizes the importance of striking a balance between risk and reward, fostering a risk-aware culture, and embracing adaptability in the face of unforeseen events. As we delve deeper into this subject, we will uncover invaluable insights on how to handle risk to achieve resilience, and growth in this ever-changing world.

Chapter 1

Understanding Risk

Understanding risk involves recognizing the potential for uncertain events or outcomes that could impact an individual, organization, or society. Risk is an inherent part of life, and it exists in various forms, including financial, operational, strategic, environmental, and personal risks.

Here are some key aspects of understanding risk:

1. Probability: Risk is often associated with the probability of an event occurring. High-probability risks are more likely to happen, while low-probability risks are less likely but could have severe consequences.

2. Impact: The impact of a risk refers to the extent of its consequences if it materializes. High-impact risks can lead to significant losses, while low-impact risks might have minimal consequences.

3. Risk Appetite: Different individuals and organizations have varying levels of risk appetite, representing the amount of risk they are willing to tolerate to achieve their goals.

4. Risk Tolerance: Risk tolerance relates to the level of discomfort or anxiety an individual or organization can endure when facing uncertainties.

5. Risk Management: Managing risk involves identifying, analyzing, and responding to potential risks. It aims to minimize negative outcomes and maximize opportunities.

6. Types of Risk: There are several categories of risk, such as financial risk, operational risk, market risk, reputational risk, and more. Each type requires specific approaches for assessment and management.

7. Uncertainty vs. Risk: While risk involves measurable probabilities and potential impacts,

uncertainty refers to situations with unknown probabilities or ambiguous outcomes.

8. Risk vs. Reward: Risk and potential rewards are often interrelated. Higher-risk activities or investments may offer greater potential rewards, but they also come with increased uncertainty. Understanding the risk-reward tradeoff is crucial in decision-making.

9. Risk Perception: Risk perception varies among individuals and can be influenced by factors such as past experiences, emotions, cognitive biases, and cultural backgrounds. People may perceive and respond to the same risk differently.

10. Systemic Risk: Systemic risk refers to risks that can cause widespread disruption in an entire system or market, affecting multiple interconnected entities simultaneously. Examples include financial crises or pandemics.

11. Risk Communication: Effectively communicating risks is essential in both personal

and professional contexts. Transparent and clear communication helps stakeholders understand potential threats and fosters trust and collaboration.

12. Risk Analysis Tools: Various quantitative and qualitative tools are used to analyze and assess risks. Some common methods include risk matrices, fault trees, scenario analysis, and Monte Carlo simulations.

13. Risk and Innovation: Embracing risk is often a prerequisite for innovation and growth. By taking calculated risks and learning from failures, individuals and organizations can explore new opportunities and stay competitive.

14. Risk Governance: Risk governance involves establishing clear roles, responsibilities, and processes for risk management within an organization. It ensures that risk-related decisions are aligned with strategic objectives.

15. Emotional Intelligence and Risk: Emotional intelligence plays a significant role in handling risk, as it helps individuals manage emotions, stay resilient in the face of challenges, and make more rational decisions.

16. Risk in Decision Making: Understanding risk is integral to effective decision-making. Identifying and evaluating risks alongside potential benefits allows for well-informed and balanced choices.

17. Risk Culture: The risk culture within an organization influences how individuals perceive and handle risk. A positive risk culture encourages risk-awareness, open communication, and continuous improvement.

Overall, a comprehensive grasp of risk entails recognizing its multidimensional nature and understanding its impact on various aspects of life. By fostering a risk-informed mindset, individuals and organizations can navigate uncertainties more adeptly, seize opportunities, and build resilience to adapt to an ever-changing world.

Importance of managing Risk

Managing risk is of paramount importance in both personal and professional realms due to the following reasons:

1. Minimizing Losses: Effective risk management helps reduce the likelihood and impact of negative outcomes. By identifying potential threats and taking appropriate measures, individuals and organizations can prevent or mitigate losses.

2. Enhancing Resilience: A robust risk management strategy enhances resilience by enabling quick recovery from adverse events. Being prepared for contingencies allows individuals and businesses to bounce back and continue operations smoothly.

3. Decision Making: A thorough understanding of risks informs better decision-making. When evaluating options, considering potential risks and

rewards helps make more informed and balanced choices.

4. Protecting Reputation: Managing risks, especially reputational risks, safeguards an individual's or organization's image and credibility. A tarnished reputation can have severe consequences on trust and public perception.

5. Seizing Opportunities: Risk management is not solely about avoiding negative outcomes; it also involves embracing calculated risks to pursue opportunities. A well-managed risk strategy can lead to innovation and growth.

6. Regulatory Compliance: Many industries and sectors have specific regulations and compliance requirements related to risk management. Adhering to these standards ensures legal and ethical conduct.

7. Financial Stability: Effective risk management in financial matters, such as investments or loans,

ensures stability and safeguards against potential financial crises.

8. Business Continuity: For organizations, risk management is crucial for maintaining business continuity during unexpected events, such as natural disasters or market disruptions.

9. Employee Safety: In workplaces, risk management is vital for ensuring the safety and well-being of employees. Identifying and mitigating workplace hazards reduces accidents and injuries.

10. Stakeholder Confidence: Stakeholders, including customers, investors, and partners, gain confidence in an organization that demonstrates a proactive and well-executed risk management approach.

11. Long-term Success: Consistent risk management fosters sustainability and longevity. By addressing risks in a systematic manner,

individuals and businesses can position themselves for long-term success.

12. Project Success: In project management, identifying and managing risks throughout the project lifecycle contributes to its success by minimizing delays and cost overruns.

In summary, managing risks is fundamental for achieving resilience, ensuring stability, making sound decisions, and fostering growth. It is a proactive and essential practice that empowers individuals and organizations to navigate uncertainties, protect
assets, and seize opportunities to thrive in an ever-changing world.

Chapter 2

Identifying Risks

Identifying risks is the foundational step in effective risk management. It involves systematically recognizing potential uncertainties that could impact objectives, projects, or activities. Here are some key methods to identify risks:

1. Brainstorming: Gather a diverse group of stakeholders and encourage open discussions to identify possible risks. Brainstorming sessions foster creative thinking and uncover various perspectives.

2. Past Data Analysis: Analyze historical data and past experiences to identify recurring patterns or events that have led to negative outcomes.

3. SWOT Analysis: Conduct a SWOT (Strengths, Weaknesses, Opportunities, Threats) analysis to identify internal and external factors that could pose risks to an organization or project.

4. Scenario Planning: Envision various scenarios, including best-case, worst-case, and most likely outcomes. This helps identify risks associated with each scenario.

5. Expert Input: Seek advice from subject matter experts or professionals who possess specialized knowledge and experience related to the area of concern.

6. Risk Registers: Use risk registers or databases to systematically document identified risks along with their potential impacts and probabilities.

7. Feedback and Lessons Learned: Review feedback from previous projects or activities and learn from past mistakes and successes to identify potential risks in future endeavors.

8. External Factors Analysis: Consider external factors such as changes in the market, regulatory environment, geopolitical landscape, or

technological advancements that could impact operations.

9. Benchmarking: Compare your practices with industry benchmarks to identify potential gaps or areas of concern that might pose risks.

10. Risk Checklists: Utilize checklists specific to your industry or domain to ensure comprehensive coverage of potential risks.

11. Simulation and Modeling: Employ simulations or models to test scenarios and assess their impact on the system or project.

12. Feedback from Stakeholders: Seek input from stakeholders, including customers, employees, and partners, as they might identify risks that others may overlook.

It's important to note that risk identification should be an ongoing process, and risks may evolve. Regularly reviewing and updating the risk assessment is crucial to stay proactive and responsive to changing circumstances.

Types of Risks

There are various types of risks that individuals, organizations, and societies face. Here are some common types of risks:

1. Financial Risk: This type of risk relates to potential losses in financial transactions or investments due to market fluctuations, credit defaults, currency fluctuations, or interest rate changes.

2. Operational Risk: Operational risks stem from internal processes, systems, or human errors that can lead to disruptions, inefficiencies, or financial losses within an organization.

3. Market Risk: Market risks arise from changes in market conditions, such as supply and demand fluctuations, price volatility, and economic uncertainties, which can impact the value of assets or investments.

4. Reputational Risk: Reputational risks refer to the potential damage to an individual's or organization's reputation due to negative publicity, public perception, or ethical issues.

5. Compliance Risk: Compliance risks arise from failure to comply with laws, regulations, or industry standards, leading to legal consequences, penalties, or reputational damage.

6. Cybersecurity Risk: Cybersecurity risks involve potential threats to an organization's digital infrastructure and data from cyberattacks, data breaches, or unauthorized access.

7. Environmental Risk: Environmental risks pertain to potential harm to the environment, ecosystem, or human health resulting from an organization's activities or natural disasters.

8. Strategic Risk: Strategic risks occur when an organization's strategic decisions or actions fail to

achieve desired outcomes or when the competitive landscape changes unexpectedly.

9. Legal Risk: Legal risks involve potential legal liabilities, lawsuits, or disputes arising from contracts, intellectual property infringements, or regulatory violations.

10. Political Risk: Political risks arise from changes in political stability, government policies, or geopolitical events that can affect businesses or investments in a region or country.

11. Technological Risk: Technological risks relate to potential disruptions or vulnerabilities resulting from the adoption or reliance on new technologies or systems.

12. Social Risk: Social risks involve potential backlash or negative impacts from an organization's social practices, such as labor issues, community relations, or cultural sensitivities.

It's important to note that these risks can be interconnected, and addressing one type of risk may influence others. Effective risk management requires a comprehensive understanding of these risks and the implementation of suitable strategies to mitigate their impact on objectives and activities.

Analyzing Potential Risks

Analyzing potential risks is a critical step in the risk management process. It involves evaluating identified risks to understand their potential impact and likelihood of occurrence. Here's how to analyze potential risks effectively:

1. Risk Probability: Assess the likelihood of each risk occurring. Use historical data, expert opinions, and statistical methods to estimate the probability of an event happening.

2. Risk Impact: Determine the potential consequences of each risk if it were to materialize. Consider the financial, operational, reputational, and other impacts on the objectives or activities.

3. Risk Severity: Combine the probability and impact assessments to rank the risks in terms of severity. This helps prioritize which risks need immediate attention and which ones can be monitored.

4. Risk Exposure: Calculate the risk exposure for each identified risk, which is the product of probability and impact. This metric helps quantify the overall potential loss associated with risk.

5. Risk Mitigation: Explore and evaluate strategies to reduce the likelihood or impact of each risk. Identify preventive measures, controls, and contingency plans to manage the risks effectively.

6. Cost-Benefit Analysis: Perform a cost-benefit analysis to determine the most suitable risk management strategies. Assess whether the cost of implementing risk mitigation measures justifies the potential reduction in risk.

7. Scenario Analysis: Conduct scenario analysis by simulating different risk scenarios to understand their potential implications on the project or business.

8. Risk Interdependencies: Examine how risks might interact with each other. Some risks can trigger or exacerbate others, leading to cascading effects.

9. Historical Comparisons: Compare current risk assessments with past risk events to draw insights and learn from previous experiences.

10. Risk Tolerance: Consider the risk tolerance level of the stakeholders involved. Different individuals or organizations may have varying levels of willingness to take on risk.

11. Sensitivity Analysis: Perform sensitivity analysis to understand how changes in key variables or assumptions can impact the severity of risks.

12. Risk Appetite Alignment: Ensure that the risk management strategies align with the organization's risk appetite, as defined by its goals and risk tolerance.

By thoroughly analyzing potential risks, individuals and organizations can make well-informed decisions, allocate resources effectively, and implement appropriate risk management measures to navigate uncertainties with greater confidence and preparedness.

Chapter 3

Risk Mitigation Strategy

Risk mitigation strategy refers to the set of actions and measures taken to reduce the impact and likelihood of identified risks. It aims to minimize the adverse consequences of potential uncertainties and enhance an individual's or organization's ability to manage challenges effectively. Here are some common risk mitigation strategies:

1. Avoidance: The most straightforward strategy is to avoid the risk altogether. This involves refraining from activities or decisions that could lead to potential risks. While effective, avoidance may limit opportunities for growth and innovation.

2. Transfer: Transferring risk involves shifting the responsibility for managing the risk to another party. This can be done through insurance, contracts, or outsourcing certain activities to specialized firms.

3. Diversification: In financial risk management, diversification is a common strategy. It involves spreading investments across various assets or industries to reduce exposure to a single risk.

4. Contingency Planning: Developing contingency plans prepares individuals and organizations to respond swiftly to adverse events. These plans outline predefined actions and resources required to mitigate the impact of specific risks.

5. Redundancy: Introducing redundancy into critical systems or processes can provide backup mechanisms in case of failures. Redundancy increases system reliability and ensures continuity of operations.

6. Safety Measures: Implementing safety protocols and training programs enhances safety and reduces the likelihood of accidents and injuries.

7. Technological Upgrades: Upgrading technology infrastructure and implementing cybersecurity measures can protect against data breaches and technological risks.

8. Compliance and Governance: Adhering to regulatory requirements and ethical standards helps mitigate legal and reputational risks.

9. Risk Awareness and Training: Educating employees and stakeholders about potential risks fosters a risk-aware culture and ensures everyone understands their role in risk management.

10. Stress Testing: Stress testing involves subjecting systems or processes to extreme scenarios to evaluate their resilience and identify potential weaknesses.

11. Early Warning Systems: Implementing early warning systems allows for timely detection and response to emerging risks.

12. Crisis Communication Plans: Developing communication plans in advance ensures a prompt and transparent response to crises, protecting reputation and stakeholder trust.

13. Insurance: Obtaining appropriate insurance coverage can provide financial protection against various risks, such as property damage, liability, and business interruption.

14. Business Continuity Planning: Business continuity plans outline procedures to ensure essential functions can continue during disruptive events.

15. Data Backup and Recovery: Regular data backup and recovery strategies safeguard against data loss from technological failures or cyberattacks.

16. Training and Skill Development: Enhancing employees' skills and knowledge helps reduce human error and increases organizational resilience.

17. Supply Chain Management: Diversifying suppliers and establishing strong supplier relationships mitigate risks related to supply chain disruptions.

18. Market Research and Analysis: Conducting thorough market research and analysis helps identify potential market risks and enables informed decision-making.

By implementing risk mitigation strategies tailored to specific risks, individuals and organizations can minimize the negative impacts of uncertainties while seizing opportunities for growth and success. Effective risk mitigation enhances resilience and ensures stability in the face of ever-changing and dynamic environments.

Avoiding Risks

Avoiding risks is a risk mitigation strategy that involves refraining from activities or decisions that could expose individuals or organizations to potential uncertainties. The goal is to eliminate the possibility of adverse consequences by not engaging in actions that carry significant risks. Here are some key aspects of avoiding risks:

1. Risk Assessment: To effectively avoid risks, individuals and organizations must conduct thorough risk assessments. Identifying potential risks and understanding their potential impact and likelihood of occurrence is crucial for informed decision-making.

2. Risk Tolerance: Establishing a risk tolerance level is essential. This involves determining the level of risk an individual or organization is willing to accept. A low-risk tolerance might lead to a more conservative approach, while a higher risk tolerance could result in a willingness to take on more uncertainty.

3. Cost-Benefit Analysis: When considering risk avoidance, a cost-benefit analysis is necessary. Assessing the potential benefits of an activity against the potential risks helps in determining whether avoidance is the best approach.

4. Opportunity Costs: While avoiding risks may offer safety and security, it might also lead to missed opportunities. Weighing the potential gains that could be sacrificed by avoiding risks is critical.

5. Strategic Decision-Making: Avoiding risks requires strategic decision-making. Identifying the core objectives and aligning actions with long-term goals can help in prioritizing risk avoidance measures.

6. Insurance: For certain risks that cannot be entirely avoided, insurance coverage provides financial protection against potential losses.

7. Compliance: Ensuring compliance with relevant laws, regulations, and industry standards is a way of avoiding legal and regulatory risks.

8. Due Diligence: Thoroughly researching and investigating potential risks before making

decisions can prevent engaging in activities with high-risk profiles.

9. Stakeholder Communication: Transparently communicating decisions and reasons for avoiding specific risks help manage expectations and build enough trust among stakeholders.

10. Long-Term Impact: Considering the long-term impact of risk avoidance decisions is essential. Short-term avoidance might lead to higher risk exposure later if critical issues aren't addressed promptly.

While avoiding risks may offer a sense of security, it is essential to balance risk avoidance with the pursuit of opportunities for growth and innovation. Total risk avoidance is often impractical or may result in missed chances for success. A balanced risk management approach involves a combination of risk avoidance, risk mitigation, risk transfer, and risk acceptance strategies tailored to the specific context and objectives of an individual or organization.

Transferring Risks

Transferring risks is a risk mitigation strategy that involves shifting the responsibility for managing potential uncertainties to another party. By doing so, individuals or organizations can reduce their exposure to specific risks and protect themselves from potential financial losses or liabilities. Here are some key aspects of transferring risks:

1. Insurance: One of the most common methods of risk transfer is through insurance. Purchasing insurance policies allows individuals or organizations to transfer the financial burden of potential losses to the insurance provider. Various types of insurance are available, such as property insurance, liability insurance, and professional indemnity insurance.

2. Contractual Agreements: In business transactions, risk transfer can be achieved through contractual agreements. Contractual clauses can allocate specific risks to one party, protecting the other from potential consequences.

3. Outsourcing: Outsourcing certain activities or services to third-party vendors is a way to transfer operational risks. By delegating responsibilities to specialized providers, organizations reduce the potential impact of risks associated with those activities.

4. Joint Ventures and Partnerships: Collaborating with other entities through joint ventures or partnerships can spread risks among the involved parties. This shared responsibility can provide mutual support in managing uncertainties.

5. Risk Hedging: In financial markets, risk transfer is accomplished through hedging strategies. For example, derivatives such as options and futures contracts allow investors to offset potential losses from market fluctuations.

6. Subcontracting: Within a larger project, subcontracting specific tasks or components can transfer risks associated with those elements to the subcontractors.

7. Performance Guarantees: In certain contracts, one party may require the other to provide performance guarantees or bonds to cover potential losses if contractual obligations are not met.

8. Indemnification: Indemnification clauses in contracts specify that one party agrees to cover the costs or losses incurred by the other party due to specified risks or events.

9. Risk Pooling: In some cases, individuals or organizations may form risk pools to collectively share risks and distribute potential losses among the participants.

10. Reinsurance: For insurance companies, reinsurance is a method of risk transfer. Reinsurers take on a portion of an insurance company's risk in exchange for a premium, reducing the insurer's exposure to large claims.

Transferring risks can be an effective strategy to safeguard against potential financial burdens and liabilities. However, it is essential to carefully assess the terms and conditions of risk transfer arrangements, understand the limitations, and consider the costs involved. Additionally, not all risks can be easily transferred, and some may require a combination of risk management strategies, including avoidance, mitigation, and acceptance, to create a comprehensive and balanced risk management approach.

Reducing Risks

Reducing risks is a risk mitigation strategy aimed at minimizing the likelihood and impact of potential uncertainties. It involves implementing measures and actions to proactively address identified risks. By reducing risks, individuals and organizations can enhance their resilience, improve decision-making, and increase the likelihood of successful outcomes. Here are some key aspects of reducing risks:

1. Risk Assessment: Conducting a comprehensive risk assessment is the starting point for risk reduction. Identifying potential risks and understanding their characteristics allows for targeted risk reduction strategies.

2. Risk Prioritization: Prioritizing risks based on their potential impact and likelihood helps in allocating resources effectively. Focusing on high-priority risks enables efficient risk-reduction efforts.

3. Risk Mitigation Plans: Developing risk mitigation plans outlines the specific actions and measures to address identified risks. These plans provide a roadmap for risk reduction activities.

4. Implementing Safety Measures: In various contexts, implementing safety protocols, guidelines, and training programs can prevent accidents, injuries, and other potential hazards.

5. Quality Control: Ensuring stringent quality control measures in manufacturing and production

processes can minimize the risk of defective products or services.

6. Technology Upgrades: Keeping technology infrastructure up to date and secure helps reduce the risk of technological failures, data breaches, and cyberattacks.

7. Contingency Planning: Developing contingency plans prepares individuals and organizations to respond effectively to unexpected events, mitigating their impact.

8. Process Optimization: Optimizing operational processes and workflows can reduce inefficiencies, minimize errors, and enhance overall risk management.

9. Training and Skill Development: Providing training and skill development opportunities to employees enhances their abilities to handle risks effectively.

10. Environmental Management: Implementing sustainable practices and environmental management strategies can reduce environmental risks and promote ecological stewardship.

11. Regulatory Compliance: Complying with relevant laws and regulations helps reduce legal and compliance risks.

12. Supply Chain Management: Developing strong supply chain relationships and diversifying suppliers can mitigate risks related to supply chain disruptions.

13. Stress Testing: Conducting stress tests on systems and processes helps identify weaknesses and vulnerabilities, enabling appropriate risk reduction measures.

14. Employee Engagement: Engaging employees in risk management efforts fosters a risk-aware culture and encourages proactive risk reduction.

15. Monitoring and Review: Continuous monitoring and review of risk reduction strategies allow for timely adjustments and improvements based on changing circumstances.

By implementing effective risk reduction strategies, individuals and organizations can proactively address potential uncertainties and minimize their exposure to adverse events. Risk reduction is an ongoing process that requires vigilance and adaptability to maintain a proactive approach to risk management and enhance overall resilience.

Accepting Risks

Accepting risks is a risk management strategy where individuals or organizations choose not to implement specific actions to mitigate potential uncertainties. Instead, they consciously decide to bear the consequences if the identified risks materialize. Accepting risks is a viable approach when the associated costs and efforts of risk mitigation outweigh the potential benefits or when certain risks are deemed an inherent part of pursuing specific objectives. Here are some key aspects of accepting risks:

1. Risk Tolerance: Accepting risks requires a clear understanding of an individual's or organization's risk tolerance level. It involves evaluating the level of risk they are willing to bear in pursuit of their goals.

2. Cost-Benefit Analysis: Conducting a cost-benefit analysis is crucial when considering risk acceptance. This analysis compares the potential benefits of pursuing an opportunity against the potential losses from not mitigating specific risks.

3. Risk Control Measures: While accepting risks, it is essential to put in place measures to monitor and control the identified risks. Establishing early warning systems and contingency plans can help minimize the impact if risks materialize.

4. Probability and Severity: Assessing the probability and severity of potential risks can aid

in deciding which risks are acceptable. Low probability or low-impact risks might be deemed acceptable without further mitigation efforts.

5. Risk Transparency: Transparency is essential when accepting risks, especially when involving stakeholders. Being upfront about the identified risks and the decision to accept them helps manage expectations and build trust.

6. Unavoidable Risks: Some risks may be unavoidable, especially in certain industries or activities. Accepting these risks might be the only practical option, and strategies to mitigate their impact may not be feasible.

7. Innovation and Growth: Accepting certain risks is often necessary for innovation and growth. Pursuing new opportunities involves venturing into uncharted territory, which inherently carries some level of uncertainty.

8. Risk Resilience: By accepting certain risks, individuals and organizations build risk resilience.

This approach acknowledges that setbacks might occur but focuses on the ability to recover and adapt.

9. Compliance with Regulations: In some cases, regulatory or legal constraints may limit the ability to fully mitigate certain risks. Accepting these risks while complying with relevant laws is essential.

10. Risk Versus Reward: Accepting risks is often a trade-off between potential rewards and potential losses. Carefully evaluating this balance helps make informed decisions.

It's important to note that accepting risks doesn't imply neglecting risk management altogether. Effective risk management involves a combination of risk acceptance, risk avoidance, risk reduction, and risk transfer strategies, depending on the specific context and objectives. Striking the right balance between accepting risks and mitigating them is key to making well-informed decisions and achieving sustainable success in a dynamic and uncertain environment.

Chapter 4

Creating a Risk Management Plan

Creating a risk management plan is a systematic approach to identifying, assessing, and managing potential risks that could impact an individual's or organization's objectives. A well-structured risk management plan helps in making informed decisions, prioritizing resources, and enhancing overall resilience. Here are the key steps to create a risk management plan:

1. Risk Identification: Start by identifying potential risks relevant to the specific context and objectives. Engage stakeholders from different departments to gather diverse perspectives. Use techniques like brainstorming, SWOT analysis, and historical data analysis to identify risks comprehensively.

2. Risk Assessment: Evaluate the impact and likelihood of each identified risk. Use qualitative and quantitative methods to prioritize risks based on their significance. Develop a risk scoring

system to compare risks and assign a level of priority to each.

3. Risk Mitigation Strategies: Based on the risk assessment, develop specific risk mitigation strategies for high-priority risks. This may include risk avoidance, risk reduction, risk transfer, and risk acceptance strategies, as appropriate.

4. Risk Mitigation Action Plan: Outline detailed action plans for implementing the identified risk mitigation strategies. Assign responsibilities, set deadlines, and establish clear communication channels to ensure effective execution.

5. Contingency Planning: Develop contingency plans to address potential risks that cannot be fully mitigated. Contingency plans outline the steps to be taken if a high-impact risk materializes, ensuring a prompt and effective response.

6. Risk Monitoring and Reporting: Establish a monitoring and reporting system to regularly assess the effectiveness of risk management

measures. Define key performance indicators (KPIs) to track progress and trigger alerts if risks escalate.

7. Stakeholder Communication: Communicate the risk management plan to relevant stakeholders, including employees, management, investors, and regulatory authorities. Ensure transparency and encourage feedback for continuous improvement.

8. Risk Management Culture: Foster a risk-aware culture within the organization by promoting risk consciousness and accountability at all levels. Encourage employees to report potential risks and actively participate in risk management efforts.

9. Risk Documentation: Document all aspects of the risk management plan, including risk identification, assessment, mitigation strategies, action plans, and monitoring procedures. A well-documented plan ensures consistency and facilitates future updates.

10. Regular Reviews and Updates: Conduct periodic reviews of the risk management plan to assess its effectiveness and make necessary updates. Risk management is an ongoing process, and the plan should evolve as the risk landscape changes.

11. Training and Awareness: Provide training and awareness programs to educate employees and stakeholders about the risk management plan and their roles in its execution.

12. Integration with Strategic Planning: Integrate the risk management plan with the organization's strategic planning process to align risk management with overall objectives and decision-making.

By following these steps, individuals and organizations can create a comprehensive and tailored risk management plan that addresses potential uncertainties, enhances preparedness, and facilitates effective decision-making in a dynamic and unpredictable environment.

Setting goals

Setting goals in a risk management plan is crucial for aligning risk management efforts with the overall objectives of an individual or organization. Clear and specific goals provide direction and focus, helping to prioritize resources and ensure that risk management activities are purposeful and effective. Here are the key steps to set goals in a risk management plan:

1. Understand Objectives: Begin by understanding the broader objectives of the individual or organization. These objectives could relate to financial performance, operational efficiency, market expansion, reputation management, or any other strategic goals.

2. Identify Risk-Related Goals: Based on the overall objectives, identify specific risk-related goals that need to be achieved. These goals should be directly related to managing uncertainties that could impact the achievement of the broader objectives.

3. Be Specific and Measurable: Ensure that each risk-related goal is specific and measurable. Clearly define the desired outcome and establish quantifiable metrics to track progress and success.

4. Prioritize Goals: Prioritize risk-related goals based on their significance and impact on the overall objectives. High-priority goals should receive more attention and resources in the risk management plan.

5. Set Realistic Timeframes: Establish realistic timeframes for achieving each goal. Consider the complexity of the risk management activities required and the resources available when setting the deadlines.

6. Address Different Risk Types: Set goals to address different types of risks, such as financial risks, operational risks, compliance risks, reputational risks, and strategic risks. Each type of risk may require different approaches and strategies.

7. Incorporate Risk Tolerance: Consider the risk tolerance level of the individual or organization when setting goals. Some risks may be accepted up to a certain threshold, while others require proactive mitigation.

8. Establish Accountability: Assign responsibility for achieving each goal to specific individuals or teams. Clearly define roles and responsibilities to ensure accountability in implementing risk management measures.

9. Integrate with Strategic Planning: Integrate risk-related goals with the organization's strategic planning process. Ensure that risk management is viewed as an integral part of decision-making and not a separate or isolated activity.

10. Align with Stakeholder Expectations: Consider the expectations and requirements of stakeholders, such as investors, customers, employees, and regulatory authorities. Align

risk-related goals with stakeholder interests and concerns.

11. Regularly Review and Update: Review the progress of risk-related goals regularly and update them as needed. Risk management is an iterative process, and goals may need adjustments based on changing circumstances and new insights.

12. Measure and Communicate Success: Measure the success of achieving risk-related goals and communicate the outcomes to stakeholders. Celebrate achievements and use lessons learned to improve future risk management efforts.

By setting clear and relevant goals in the risk management plan, individuals and organizations can proactively address uncertainties, enhance decision-making, and increase the likelihood of achieving their overall objectives in a risk-aware and resilient manner.

Assessing Risk Tolerance

Assessing risk tolerance is a critical step in risk management, as it helps individuals and organizations understand their willingness and capacity to take on uncertainties. Risk tolerance is the level of risk that an individual or organization is comfortable with and can afford to bear without jeopardizing their financial well-being or objectives. Here are the key factors and steps involved in assessing risk tolerance:

1. Financial Capacity: Evaluate the financial capacity to absorb potential losses. Consider factors such as available funds, cash reserves, and the ability to recover from financial setbacks.

2. Goals and Objectives: Understand the specific goals and objectives of the individual or organization. Risk tolerance may vary depending on whether the primary focus is on capital preservation, growth, income generation, or a combination of these goals.

3. Time Horizon: Consider the time horizon for the investment or project. Longer time horizons

typically allow for higher risk tolerance, as there is more time to recover from short-term fluctuations.

4. Experience and Expertise: Assess the individual's or organization's experience and expertise in dealing with risk. Those with more knowledge and experience may have a higher risk tolerance, as they are better equipped to handle uncertainties.

5. Risk Perception: Understand how the individual or organization perceives risk. Risk perception can be influenced by personal beliefs, experiences, and biases.

6. Risk Capacity: Differentiate between risk tolerance and risk capacity. While risk tolerance is about the willingness to take on risk, risk capacity focuses on the ability to handle risk based on financial resources.

7. Age and Life Stage: Consider the age and life stage of the individual or organization. Younger

individuals or organizations may have higher risk tolerance as they have more time to recover from potential losses.

8. External Factors: Analyze external factors such as economic conditions, market trends, and regulatory environment. These factors can influence risk tolerance over time.

9. Risk Tolerance Questionnaires: Use risk tolerance questionnaires to gauge the individual's or organization's attitude towards risk. These questionnaires can provide valuable insights into risk preferences.

10. Consultation with Professionals: Seek advice from financial advisors, risk management experts, or consultants. Professionals can provide an objective perspective and help in understanding risk tolerance in a broader context.

11. Stress Testing: Conduct stress tests to evaluate the reaction to different scenarios of risk and market volatility. Stress testing helps assess how

much risk an individual or organization can tolerate without making impulsive decisions.

12. Reassessment and Review: Regularly reassess risk tolerance as circumstances change. Life events, market conditions, and financial situations can impact risk tolerance over time.

By carefully assessing risk tolerance, individuals and organizations can align their risk management strategies with their comfort level and financial capacity. This helps in making informed decisions about risk-taking, investment choices, and overall risk management approaches. Understanding risk tolerance is essential for creating a well-balanced and effective risk management plan that suits the specific needs and objectives of the individual or organization.

Developing Response strategies

Developing response strategies is a crucial component of a risk management plan. These strategies outline specific actions and measures to address identified risks effectively. By developing response strategies, individuals and organizations can be better prepared to mitigate the impact of uncertainties and seize opportunities. Here are the key steps to develop response strategies:

1. Risk Assessment: Start by conducting a thorough risk assessment to identify and understand potential risks. Evaluate the impact and likelihood of each risk to prioritize response efforts.

2. Risk Prioritization: Prioritize risks based on their significance and potential impact on objectives. Focus on high-priority risks that require immediate attention and resources.

3. Risk Mitigation Options: For each high-priority risk, explore different risk mitigation options. Consider risk avoidance, risk reduction, risk transfer, and risk acceptance strategies as appropriate.

4. Action Plan Development: Create a detailed action plan for each selected response strategy.

Outline the steps to be taken, responsibilities, timelines, and required resources.

5. Contingency Planning: Develop contingency plans to address risks that cannot be fully mitigated. Contingency plans outline predefined actions to be taken if high-impact risks materialize.

6. Resource Allocation: Allocate resources effectively to implement the response strategies. Ensure that sufficient resources are allocated to manage high-priority risks.

7. Communication Plan: Establish a communication plan to ensure that all stakeholders are informed about the response strategies and their roles in executing them.

8. Test and Simulation: Conduct tests and simulations of response strategies to assess their effectiveness. Testing helps identify potential gaps and areas for improvement.

9. Flexibility and Adaptability: Design response strategies with flexibility and adaptability in mind. Recognize that risks and circumstances may change, and response plans may need adjustments.

10. Integration with Business Processes: Integrate response strategies into existing business processes and decision-making frameworks. Ensure that risk management becomes an integral part of day-to-day operations.

11. Employee Training: Provide training to employees and stakeholders involved in executing response strategies. Ensure they are equipped with the necessary skills and knowledge to implement the plans effectively.

12. Monitoring and Review: Establish a monitoring and review mechanism to assess the progress and effectiveness of response strategies. Regularly review the response plans and update them as needed.

13. Communication and Coordination: Foster communication and coordination among relevant teams and departments to ensure a cohesive approach to risk response.

14. Resource and Budget Allocation: Allocate appropriate resources and budget to implement the response strategies effectively.

15. Risk Owner Identification: Assign risk owners who are responsible for overseeing the execution of response strategies and ensuring accountability.

By developing response strategies, individuals and organizations can enhance their ability to manage uncertainties, protect against potential losses, and capitalize on opportunities. Effective response strategies are essential for creating a resilient and proactive risk management approach that aligns with overall objectives and enhances the likelihood of successful outcomes.

Chapter 5

Implementing Risk Management Practices

Implementing risk management practices is a dynamic process that involves integrating risk management principles into an individual's or organization's day-to-day operations and decision-making. Successful implementation requires commitment, communication, and a risk-aware culture. Here are the key steps to effectively implement risk management practices:

1. Leadership Support: Obtain buy-in and support from top management and leadership. Leaders should champion the importance of risk management and allocate necessary resources for its successful implementation.

2. Establish a Risk Management Team: Form a dedicated risk management team or designate individuals responsible for overseeing risk management activities. This team should include representatives from different departments to ensure a comprehensive approach.

3. Develop a Risk Management Policy: Create a clear and concise risk management policy that outlines the organization's commitment to risk management, roles and responsibilities, and the overall approach to managing uncertainties.

4. Identify and Assess Risks: Conduct a comprehensive risk assessment to identify potential risks that could impact the organization's objectives. Evaluate the impact and likelihood of each risk to prioritize risk management efforts.

5. Develop Response Strategies: Based on the risk assessment, develop response strategies to address identified risks. Consider risk avoidance, risk reduction, risk transfer, and risk acceptance as appropriate.

6. Integrate Risk Management into Processes: Integrate risk management practices into existing business processes, strategic planning, project management, and decision-making frameworks. This ensures that risk considerations are ingrained in the organization's DNA.

7. Communication and Training: Communicate the importance of risk management to all employees and stakeholders. Provide training to employees involved in risk management to enhance their understanding and skills.

8. Implement Risk Monitoring and Reporting: Establish a risk monitoring and reporting system to track the progress of response strategies and identify emerging risks. Regularly report risk-related information to relevant stakeholders.

9. Establish a Risk Register: Maintain a risk register or database to document identified risks, their impact assessments, and response plans. This central repository ensures all risks are accounted for and can be reviewed periodically.

10. Regular Review and Updates: Continuously review and update risk management practices to adapt to changing circumstances, new risks, and lessons learned from previous experiences.

11. Risk Culture and Awareness: Foster a risk-aware culture where all employees are encouraged to identify and report potential risks. Create an environment that values risk management and sees it as a collaborative effort.

12. Monitor Risk Management Performance: Evaluate the effectiveness of implemented risk management practices regularly. Use key performance indicators (KPIs) to measure progress and identify areas for improvement.

13. Continuous Improvement: Emphasize a culture of continuous improvement in risk management. Encourage feedback and suggestions from employees to enhance risk management practices.

By implementing risk management practices effectively, individuals and organizations can proactively address uncertainties, protect against potential losses, and capitalize on opportunities. Successful risk management integration helps in achieving objectives, ensuring sustainability, and enhancing overall resilience in an ever-changing and unpredictable environment.

Integrating with projects

Integrating risk management with projects is essential to ensure that potential uncertainties are addressed proactively throughout the project's lifecycle. By incorporating risk management practices into project management processes, individuals and organizations can increase the chances of project success, minimize disruptions, and improve decision-making. Here are the key steps to integrate risk management with projects:

1. Risk Identification: Begin by identifying potential risks specific to the project. Engage project team members, stakeholders, and subject matter experts to gather diverse perspectives on potential uncertainties.

2. Risk Assessment: Evaluate the impact and likelihood of each identified risk on the project's objectives. Prioritize risks based on their significance and potential to affect project success.

3. Risk Response Planning: Develop specific risk response plans for high-priority risks. Consider risk avoidance, risk reduction, risk transfer, and risk acceptance strategies to address identified risks.

4. Risk Mitigation in Project Planning: Integrate risk mitigation strategies into the project plan. Adjust the project schedule, budget, and scope to account for potential risks and response actions.

5. Contingency Planning: Develop contingency plans to address risks that cannot be fully mitigated. These plans outline predefined actions to be taken if high-impact risks materialize during the project.

6. Risk Owner Assignment: Assign risk owners who will be responsible for overseeing the execution of risk response plans and monitoring risk factors throughout the project.

7. Risk Monitoring and Reporting: Regularly monitor and update risk registers or risk databases. Report on risk status and response actions to project stakeholders as part of regular project progress updates.

8. Decision-Making with Risk Considerations: Incorporate risk considerations into project decision-making processes. Evaluate alternative approaches based on their risk profiles and potential impact on project success.

9. Communication and Collaboration: Foster open communication and collaboration among project team members to ensure that risk information is shared effectively and response actions are coordinated.

10. Risk Review at Milestones: Conduct risk reviews at project milestones or critical decision points. Reassess risk assessments and response plans as the project progresses.

11. Lessons Learned: After project completion, conduct a comprehensive lessons learned session to capture insights and experiences related to risk management. Use this information to improve future project risk management practices.

12. Training and Awareness: Provide training to project team members on risk management concepts and practices. Ensure that all team members understand their roles in identifying and addressing risks.

By integrating risk management with projects, individuals and organizations can be better prepared to handle uncertainties and unexpected events that may arise during project execution. This proactive approach enhances the likelihood of project success, improves risk management capabilities, and contributes to overall organizational resilience.

Regular Monitoring and Evaluation
Regular monitoring and evaluation are essential components of effective risk management. By

continuously monitoring and evaluating risk management efforts, individuals and organizations can assess the effectiveness of their strategies, identify emerging risks, and make informed decisions to enhance their resilience. Here's how regular monitoring and evaluation contribute to risk management:

1. Risk Status Tracking: Regular monitoring allows individuals and organizations to track the status of identified risks and their response actions. It helps ensure that risk management measures are being implemented as planned.

2. Early Detection of Emerging Risks: Regular monitoring enables the early detection of emerging risks or changes in the risk landscape. Identifying new risks promptly allows for proactive response planning.

3. Performance Measurement: Monitoring and evaluation allow the assessment of the performance of risk management strategies. Key

performance indicators (KPIs) help measure progress and identify areas for improvement.

4. Decision-Making Support: Regular evaluations provide valuable insights that support decision-making. It helps individuals and organizations adjust risk management strategies based on changing circumstances and new information.

5. Continuous Improvement: The feedback obtained from monitoring and evaluation fosters a culture of continuous improvement in risk management practices.

6. Response Plan Updates: As new risks are identified or existing risks change, response plans can be updated accordingly through regular monitoring and evaluation.

7. Resource Allocation Optimization: By analyzing the performance of risk management strategies, resource allocation can be optimized to focus on high-impact risks.

8. Adaptability to Changing Environments: Regular monitoring and evaluation enable individuals and organizations to adapt to dynamic and uncertain environments effectively.

9. Stakeholder Communication: Reporting the results of monitoring and evaluation to stakeholders fosters transparency and builds trust. It demonstrates the commitment to proactive risk management.

10. Compliance and Regulation: Regular monitoring ensures that risk management practices comply with relevant laws, regulations, and industry standards.

11. Lessons Learned: Evaluating the outcomes of risk management efforts provides valuable lessons learned that can be applied to future projects and initiatives.

12. Risk Awareness: Regular monitoring and evaluation contribute to a risk-aware culture

within an organization, where all stakeholders understand the importance of managing uncertainties.

To effectively implement regular monitoring and evaluation, individuals and organizations should establish clear evaluation criteria, set review intervals, and involve relevant stakeholders in the process. It is an iterative process that requires ongoing commitment and dedication to continuously improve risk management practices and enhance overall risk resilience.

Chapter 6

Communication and Stakeholder Involvement

Communication and stakeholder involvement are integral components of successful risk management. Engaging stakeholders and fostering open communication are essential for identifying risks, gaining support for risk management efforts, and ensuring a shared understanding of potential uncertainties. Here's how communication and stakeholder involvement contribute to effective risk management:

1. Risk Identification: Involving stakeholders from different departments and levels of the organization enhances the identification of potential risks. Stakeholders' diverse perspectives provide a comprehensive view of the risks that could impact the organization.

2. Risk Assessment: Engaging stakeholders in risk assessment helps in evaluating the impact and likelihood of identified risks accurately. Stakeholders' input can help prioritize risks based

on their significance to various departments and overall organizational objectives.

3. Support and Buy-in: Effective communication helps in gaining support and buy-in from stakeholders for risk management initiatives. When stakeholders understand the importance of risk management, they are more likely to actively participate in risk mitigation efforts.

4. Decision-Making: Involving stakeholders in risk-related decisions ensures that risk management is integrated into organizational decision-making processes. Collaborative decision-making considers various perspectives, leading to more robust risk responses.

5. Transparency and Accountability: Transparent communication about identified risks, response strategies, and progress updates fosters accountability among stakeholders. Each stakeholder's role and responsibility in risk management become clear.

6. Risk Mitigation Implementation: Engaging stakeholders in the implementation of risk mitigation strategies improves the chances of successful execution. Stakeholders can contribute their expertise and resources to address specific risks.

7. Risk Culture: Open communication and stakeholder involvement contribute to a risk-aware culture within the organization. This culture encourages employees to proactively report potential risks and take ownership of risk management.

8. Early Warning System: Involving stakeholders in risk monitoring establishes an early warning system for emerging risks. Regular communication ensures timely identification and response to new uncertainties.

9. Reporting and Updates: Regularly communicating risk management progress and outcomes to stakeholders keeps them informed about the effectiveness of risk management

efforts. It builds trust and confidence in the organization's risk management practices.

10. Stakeholder Expectations: Understanding stakeholder expectations related to risk management helps in aligning risk management practices with organizational goals and stakeholder interests.

11. External Stakeholders: Engaging external stakeholders, such as customers, suppliers, and regulatory authorities, is crucial for addressing risks that may originate from external sources.

12. Feedback and Improvement: Encouraging feedback from stakeholders provides valuable insights for improving risk management practices. Stakeholder feedback contributes to continuous improvement in risk management strategies.

To effectively involve stakeholders and foster communication, individuals and organizations should establish clear communication channels, hold regular meetings, share risk information transparently, and actively seek feedback. Creating a collaborative risk management environment ensures that risks are addressed comprehensively, leading to enhanced resilience and successful outcomes.

Reporting Risks

Reporting risks is a crucial aspect of risk management, as it involves communicating information about identified risks, their potential impact, and the actions being taken to address them. Reporting risks allows stakeholders, including management, employees, investors, and regulatory authorities, to stay informed and make informed decisions. Here are key considerations for reporting risks effectively:

1. Clear and Concise Reporting: Ensure that risk reports are clear, concise, and easy to understand. Use language that is accessible to both technical and non-technical stakeholders.

2. Relevant Information: Include relevant information about the identified risks, such as

their description, potential consequences, likelihood of occurrence, and current risk levels.

3. Risk Categories: Categorize risks into relevant categories (e.g., financial, operational, strategic, compliance) to provide a structured overview of the risk landscape.

4. Risk Severity: Assess and report on the severity of each risk, considering the potential impact on objectives and the organization as a whole.

5. Risk Trends: Identify and report on trends related to risk occurrences, highlighting any significant changes or emerging risks.

6. Risk Response Plans: Include information about the risk response plans and actions being implemented to mitigate or address the identified risks.

7. Risk Ownership: Clearly indicate the individuals or teams responsible for overseeing

the execution of risk response plans and managing each risk.

8. Frequency of Reporting: Determine the frequency of risk reporting based on the nature of the risks and the needs of stakeholders. Some risks may require more frequent reporting than others.

9. Visual Aids: Use visual aids, such as graphs, charts, and tables, to present complex risk information in a visually appealing and easily digestible format.

10. Forward-Looking Information: Provide forward-looking information about potential risks that may arise in the future or risks that are anticipated to evolve over time.

11. Risk Status Updates: Regularly update risk status to reflect changes in risk profiles, response actions, and progress towards risk mitigation.

12. Tailored Reports: Tailor risk reports to the needs of different stakeholders. Executive-level

reports may focus on high-level risk summaries, while operational reports may provide more detailed risk information.

13. Compliance and Regulations: Ensure that risk reporting complies with relevant laws, regulations, and reporting standards, especially for publicly traded companies.

14. Two-Way Communication: Encourage two-way communication with stakeholders to solicit feedback, address concerns, and gather additional insights about potential risks.

15. Timeliness: Deliver risk reports in a timely manner to keep stakeholders informed and enable timely decision-making.

Effective risk reporting facilitates a transparent and risk-aware culture within the organization and supports proactive risk management efforts. It enhances the organization's ability to respond to uncertainties and contributes to overall risk resilience.

Engaging Stakeholders

Engaging stakeholders is a vital aspect of effective risk management, as it involves individuals or groups who have a vested interest in an organization's activities, decisions, or outcomes. Engaged stakeholders are more likely to contribute valuable insights, actively participate in risk management efforts, and support the organization's risk mitigation strategies. Here are key considerations for engaging stakeholders in risk management:

1. Identify Key Stakeholders: Identify the stakeholders who are directly or indirectly affected by the organization's activities or are involved in risk management decisions. These may include employees, customers, suppliers, investors, regulatory authorities, and the community.

2. Establish Clear Objectives: Clearly define the objectives of stakeholder engagement in risk management. Determine what information you

want to gather from stakeholders and how their input will contribute to decision-making.

3. Communication Channels: Establish effective communication channels to engage stakeholders. Utilize various communication methods such as meetings, workshops, surveys, emails, and social media to reach different stakeholders.

4. Active Listening: Actively listen to stakeholders' concerns, feedback, and perspectives on risk management. Demonstrate that their input is valued and considered in risk mitigation strategies.

5. Two-Way Communication: Encourage two-way communication to foster dialogue and collaboration. Engage in open discussions and address any questions or concerns raised by stakeholders.

6. Regular Updates: Keep stakeholders informed about risk management activities, progress, and

outcomes. Provide regular updates on risk identification, assessment, and response efforts.

7. Stakeholder Involvement in Risk Identification: Involve stakeholders in the process of identifying potential risks. Their diverse perspectives can provide valuable insights into risks that might otherwise be overlooked.

8. Collaborative Decision-Making: Collaborate with stakeholders in risk-related decision-making processes. Seek their input in developing risk response plans and strategies.

9. Training and Capacity Building: Provide training and capacity-building opportunities to stakeholders to enhance their understanding of risk management concepts and their role in the process.

10. Stakeholder-Specific Engagement: Tailor engagement approaches to the needs and preferences of different stakeholder groups.

Understand their specific interests and concerns related to risk management.

11. Regular Engagement Activities: Conduct regular engagement activities to maintain ongoing dialogue with stakeholders. Create opportunities for feedback and continuous improvement.

12. Risk Communication Transparency: Be transparent in risk communication. Provide honest and accurate information about identified risks, potential consequences, and the organization's response efforts.

13. Acknowledge Contributions: Acknowledge and appreciate the contributions of stakeholders in risk management efforts. Recognize their efforts and celebrate successful risk mitigation outcomes.

14. Use Stakeholder Input: Actively use the input and insights gathered from stakeholders in risk management decision-making. Demonstrate that stakeholder engagement makes a difference in the organization's approach to risk.

Engaging stakeholders in risk management fosters a collaborative and risk-aware culture within the organization. It enhances the effectiveness of risk management strategies, strengthens risk resilience, and builds trust and support among stakeholders. Ultimately, stakeholder engagement contributes to more informed and holistic risk management practices.

Chapter 7

Financial Risk Management

Financial risk management is the process of identifying, assessing, and mitigating financial risks that could impact an individual's or organization's financial performance, stability, and objectives. It involves various strategies and techniques to manage uncertainties related to financial markets, investments, cash flow, credit, and other financial activities. Here are some key aspects of financial risk management:

1. Types of Financial Risks: Financial risks can be broadly categorized into market risk, credit risk, liquidity risk, operational risk, and legal/regulatory risk. Each type of risk requires specific approaches for management.

2. Market Risk: Market risk relates to potential losses due to changes in financial market conditions, such as interest rates, foreign exchange rates, commodity prices, and stock market fluctuations. Hedging, diversification, and

asset-liability management are common market risk mitigation strategies.

3. Credit Risk: Credit risk refers to the risk of financial losses arising from the inability of counterparties to fulfill their financial obligations. Credit risk management involves credit analysis, setting credit limits, and collateral requirements.

4. Liquidity Risk: Liquidity risk arises from the inability to meet financial obligations when they become due. Effective liquidity risk management involves maintaining sufficient cash reserves and access to credit lines.

5. Operational Risk: Operational risk is the risk of losses resulting from internal processes, people, systems, or external events. Strong internal controls, risk assessments, and business continuity planning help mitigate operational risks.

6. Risk Assessment: Conduct a comprehensive risk assessment to identify and evaluate financial

risks. Assess the impact and likelihood of each risk to prioritize risk management efforts.

7. Risk Mitigation Strategies: Develop risk mitigation strategies tailored to the specific financial risks identified. These strategies may include risk avoidance, risk reduction, risk transfer, and risk acceptance.

8. Financial Hedging: Financial hedging involves using financial instruments like derivatives to offset potential losses from adverse price movements or interest rate fluctuations.

9. Stress Testing: Conduct stress tests to assess the financial impact of extreme scenarios on an individual's or organization's financial position.

10. Capital Adequacy: Ensure that the organization maintains adequate capital reserves to absorb unexpected losses and meet regulatory requirements.

11. Compliance and Regulation: Comply with relevant financial regulations and standards to mitigate legal and regulatory risks.

12. Reporting and Transparency: Regularly report on financial risk management activities to relevant stakeholders, including investors, board members, and regulators.

13. Risk Monitoring and Review: Continuously monitor financial risks and review risk management strategies. Adjust risk management measures as needed based on changing circumstances.

14. Financial Risk Culture: Foster a risk-aware culture within the organization to ensure that financial risk management is ingrained in decision-making processes.

15. Expertise and Training: Ensure that the organization has access to financial risk management expertise and provide training to employees involved in financial activities.

Financial risk management is a dynamic and ongoing process that requires continuous monitoring and adaptability to changing market conditions and business environments. By effectively managing financial risks, individuals and organizations can enhance their financial stability, protect assets, and make informed financial decisions.

Hedging and Diversification

Hedging and diversification are two important strategies used in financial risk management to reduce exposure to potential losses and uncertainties. Both strategies aim to protect an individual's or organization's financial assets and investments from adverse market movements or events. Here's how hedging and diversification work:

1. Hedging:
-Hedging is a risk management technique that involves using financial instruments, such as

derivatives, to offset potential losses from adverse price movements or interest rate fluctuations.

- It is commonly used to protect against market risks, such as currency risk, interest rate risk, and commodity price risk.

- The process of hedging involves taking an opposite position to an existing exposure to neutralize potential losses. For example, a company that has significant foreign currency exposure may use currency forwards or options to hedge against exchange rate fluctuations.

- By hedging, individuals and organizations can reduce the impact of unpredictable market movements on their financial positions, making their overall portfolio more stable.

2. Diversification:

- Diversification is a risk management strategy that involves spreading investments across different asset classes, industries, or geographic regions to reduce overall risk.

- The idea behind diversification is that different assets or investments may react differently to the same economic events or market conditions. As a result, losses in one investment may be offset by gains in another.

- Diversification can be achieved by investing in a mix of stocks, bonds, real estate, commodities, and other assets. It can also involve investing in companies or industries with low correlation to each other.

- By diversifying their portfolios, individuals and organizations can potentially achieve a more stable return over time and reduce the impact of any single investment's underperformance.

Both hedging and diversification have their advantages and limitations. Hedging provides targeted protection against specific risks but may involve additional costs and may not fully eliminate all risks. Diversification, on the other hand, provides a broader risk reduction by spreading investments across various assets, but it may not protect against individual asset-specific risks.

The choice between hedging and diversification depends on an individual's or organization's risk appetite, financial goals, and specific risk exposures. Many financial risk management strategies use a combination of both hedging and diversification to achieve a balanced approach and minimize overall risk while pursuing investment objectives.

Using Insurance for Risk Mitigation

Using insurance for risk mitigation is a common and effective strategy to transfer financial risks to an insurance provider. Insurance provides individuals and organizations with financial protection against various uncertainties and potential losses. Here's how insurance works as a risk mitigation tool:

1. Risk Transfer: When an individual or organization purchases insurance, they are essentially transferring the financial risk associated with a specific event to the insurance company. In exchange for regular premium payments, the insurer agrees to bear the financial burden if the insured event occurs.

2. Coverage for Specific Risks: Insurance policies are designed to cover specific risks, such as property damage, liability, business interruption, health issues, and natural disasters. Each insurance policy outlines the conditions under which the insurance company will provide compensation.

3. Financial Protection: Insurance provides financial protection by compensating for losses or damages caused by covered events. This protection can help individuals and organizations recover financially and minimize the impact of unexpected events.

4. Premium Payments: To maintain insurance coverage, the insured party must make regular premium payments to the insurance company. The premium amount is determined based on the level of risk and coverage provided.

5. Customized Policies: Insurance companies offer a range of policies that can be customized to suit the specific needs of individuals or businesses. Tailoring insurance coverage ensures that risks

unique to an individual or organization are adequately addressed.

6. Legal and Regulatory Requirements: In some cases, insurance is mandatory to comply with legal or regulatory requirements. For example, auto insurance is typically required by law in many countries.

7. Types of Insurance: There are various types of insurance available to address different risks. Common types include property insurance, liability insurance, health insurance, life insurance, and business interruption insurance.

8. Risk Transfer for Businesses: For businesses, insurance is a crucial risk management tool to protect against property damage, lawsuits, employee-related risks, and other potential financial liabilities.

9. Risk Pooling: Insurance companies pool premiums from multiple policyholders to create a fund that can be used to compensate those who

experience losses. This spreading of risk across a larger group helps reduce the financial impact on individual policyholders.

10. Limitations of Insurance: It's important to note that insurance may not cover all types of risks or may have specific exclusions. Additionally, some risks may be difficult or costly to insure, and self-insurance or other risk mitigation strategies may be more appropriate in such cases.

Using insurance for risk mitigation provides individuals and organizations with peace of mind, financial security, and the ability to focus on their objectives without being overly burdened by potential financial losses. It is essential to carefully assess insurance needs, choose appropriate coverage, and work with reputable insurance providers to ensure effective risk transfer and protection.

Chapter 8

Operational Risk Management

Operational risk management is the process of identifying, assessing, and mitigating risks arising from internal processes, people, systems, or external events that could disrupt an organization's operations or lead to financial losses. Operational risks can stem from various sources, such as human error, technological failures, fraud, supply chain disruptions, regulatory non-compliance, and natural disasters. Here are key aspects of operational risk management:

1. Risk Identification: Identify potential operational risks by analyzing the organization's processes, systems, and activities. Engage employees and stakeholders to gather insights into potential risks.

2. Risk Assessment: Evaluate the impact and likelihood of identified operational risks. Prioritize risks based on their significance and potential consequences on the organization's objectives.

3. Risk Mitigation Strategies: Develop risk mitigation strategies to address identified operational risks. Strategies may include process improvements, enhanced controls, automation, and redundancy measures.

4. Internal Controls: Implement strong internal controls to reduce the likelihood of operational failures and enhance risk management effectiveness.

5. Business Continuity Planning: Develop business continuity plans to ensure the organization can recover quickly from unexpected events and continue critical operations.

6. Fraud Prevention and Detection: Implement measures to prevent and detect fraud, such as segregation of duties, regular audits, and employee training.

7. Technology and Cybersecurity: Address technology-related risks by implementing robust

cybersecurity measures, regular software updates, and data backup protocols.

8. Supply Chain Risk Management: Assess and manage risks associated with the organization's supply chain, including dependencies on key suppliers.

9. Regulatory Compliance: Ensure compliance with relevant laws, regulations, and industry standards to mitigate compliance-related risks.

10. Incident Reporting and Monitoring: Establish a system for reporting and monitoring operational incidents. Analyze incidents to identify root causes and prevent recurrence.

11. Risk Culture: Foster a risk-aware culture within the organization, where all employees understand the importance of identifying and managing operational risks.

12. Risk Management Training: Provide training to employees on operational risk management concepts and best practices.

13. Scenario Analysis: Conduct scenario analysis to assess the potential impact of different risk scenarios and develop contingency plans accordingly.

14. Key Risk Indicators (KRIs): Establish key risk indicators to monitor the early warning signs of potential operational issues.

15. Continuous Improvement: Continuously review and improve operational risk management practices based on lessons learned and changing business environments.

Operational risk management is an ongoing and iterative process that requires a proactive approach to identify and address potential threats to the organization's operations. By effectively managing operational risks, individuals and organizations can enhance their operational resilience, protect against financial losses, and ensure the smooth functioning of critical processes and activities.

Ensuring Business Continuity

Ensuring business continuity is essential for organizations to maintain their critical operations and deliver products and services during and after disruptive events. Business continuity planning involves the development of strategies and measures to minimize the impact of potential threats and quickly recover from disruptions. Here are key steps to ensure business continuity:

1. Risk Assessment: Conduct a comprehensive risk assessment to identify potential threats and vulnerabilities that could disrupt business operations. Consider both internal and external risks, such as natural disasters, technological failures, supply chain disruptions, and cyberattacks.

2. Business Impact Analysis (BIA): Perform a business impact analysis to assess the potential consequences of different disruptive events on

critical business processes, employees, customers, and financials. The BIA helps prioritize the most critical functions and resources that require protection.

3. Business Continuity Plan (BCP) Development: Develop a well-documented and actionable business continuity plan that outlines specific strategies, response procedures, and responsibilities for different disruptive scenarios. The plan should include procedures for emergency response, communication, data backup, and recovery.

4. Redundancy and Resilience: Build redundancy and resilience into critical systems and processes. Implement backup systems, redundant infrastructure, and contingency arrangements to minimize single points of failure.

5. Employee Training and Awareness: Train employees on their roles and responsibilities during a disruptive event. Ensure they are aware

of the business continuity plan and know how to respond effectively.

6. Communication Plan: Establish a communication plan that outlines how employees, customers, suppliers, and other stakeholders will be informed during a disruption. Effective communication is critical for managing expectations and building trust.

7. Regular Testing and Exercises: Conduct regular testing and exercises to validate the effectiveness of the business continuity plan. Simulation drills help identify gaps and weaknesses and allow employees to practice their roles in a safe environment.

8. Review and Updates: Periodically review and update the business continuity plan to reflect changes in the organization's operations, technology, and risk landscape. Stay informed about emerging risks and incorporate lessons learned from past incidents.

9. Supply Chain Resilience: Collaborate with suppliers and partners to ensure supply chain resilience. Identify critical suppliers and develop contingency plans in case of supply disruptions.

10. Cloud Computing and Data Backup: Consider using cloud-based services for data storage and backup to ensure data accessibility during disruptions.

11. Crisis Management Team: Establish a crisis management team that includes key decision-makers and stakeholders. This team will be responsible for coordinating response efforts during a disruptive event.

12. Business Recovery and Restoration: Plan for business recovery and restoration activities after the immediate crisis is over. Outline steps to return to normal operations and rebuild affected areas.

13. Review Insurance Coverage: Review insurance policies to ensure they adequately cover potential risks and disruptions.

By implementing comprehensive business continuity measures, organizations can enhance their ability to withstand disruptions, maintain customer trust, and safeguard their reputation. Business continuity planning is an ongoing process that requires continuous improvement and adaptability to changing circumstances and emerging threats.

Responding to Incidence

Responding to incidents is a critical aspect of effective risk management and business continuity. Incidents can range from minor disruptions to major crises, and how an organization responds can significantly impact its ability to recover and minimize the impact of the event. Here are key steps to effectively respond to incidents:

1. Activate Incident Response Team: Immediately activate the incident response team, which may include key decision-makers, subject matter experts, and representatives from relevant departments.

2. Assess the Situation: Conduct a thorough assessment of the incident's scope, impact, and severity. Gather as much information as possible to make informed decisions.

3. Communication: Establish clear communication channels to keep all stakeholders informed about the incident, its impact, and response efforts. Communicate with employees, customers, suppliers, regulators, and the media as appropriate.

4. Prioritize Response Actions: Prioritize response actions based on the severity and urgency of the incident. Focus on protecting life, critical assets, and essential business functions.

5. Contain the Incident: Take immediate actions to contain the incident and prevent it from spreading further. This may involve isolating affected systems, securing premises, or evacuating employees if necessary.

6. Implement Business Continuity Measures: Activate the business continuity plan to ensure critical operations can continue or be quickly restored. Follow predefined recovery procedures to minimize downtime.

7. Coordinate with Relevant Authorities: If the incident involves regulatory or legal implications, coordinate with relevant authorities and comply with reporting requirements.

8. Incident Documentation: Keep detailed records of the incident response activities, decisions made, and actions taken. Documentation is crucial for post-incident analysis and improvement.

9. Invoke Crisis Management: If the incident escalates into a crisis, invoke the crisis

management team to oversee response efforts and make high-level decisions.

10. Resource Management: Allocate resources effectively to support response efforts. This may include personnel, equipment, and external support if required.

11. Regular Updates: Provide regular updates to stakeholders about the incident response progress and any changes in the situation.

12. Learn from the Incident: After the incident is under control, conduct a thorough post-incident analysis to identify lessons learned and areas for improvement. Use this information to update and strengthen incident response plans.

13. Support Employees and Stakeholders: Offer support and assistance to employees and stakeholders affected by the incident. Address their concerns and provide necessary resources for recovery.

14. Reassess and Adjust: Continuously reassess the situation and adjust response actions as needed. Be flexible and adapt to changing circumstances.

15. Debriefing: Conduct a formal debriefing session with the incident response team to gather feedback and assess the effectiveness of the response. Use this feedback to enhance future incident response capabilities.

Responding to incidents requires a well-prepared and coordinated effort. By having a robust incident response plan, clear communication, and a proactive approach, organizations can minimize the impact of incidents and maintain their resilience in the face of unexpected events.

Chapter 9

Human Factor in Risk Management

The human factor plays a crucial role in risk management as it can significantly influence how risks are identified, assessed, and mitigated within an organization. Human actions, decisions, and behaviors can both contribute to and mitigate various types of risks. Here are some key aspects of the human factor in risk management:

1. Risk Perception: How individuals perceive and interpret risks can impact the effectiveness of risk management. Some people may be risk-averse and tend to overreact to perceived risks, while others may be risk-tolerant and underestimate potential dangers.

2. Risk Identification: The ability of employees to identify and report potential risks is vital in the risk management process. Encouraging a risk-aware culture can lead to more comprehensive risk identification.

3. Human Error: Human error is a common cause of operational risks. Training employees and implementing strong internal controls can help reduce the likelihood of errors and mitigate their consequences.

4. Decision-Making: Risk management decisions made by individuals, teams, or management can shape the organization's risk exposure. Sound risk-informed decision-making is essential for effective risk management.

5. Compliance and Ethics: Compliance with policies, procedures, and regulatory requirements is essential for mitigating legal and compliance risks. Promoting ethical behavior helps minimize reputational and legal risks.

6. Training and Awareness: Providing comprehensive training and raising risk awareness among employees can improve their understanding of potential risks and how to respond to them.

7. Reporting and Communication: Encouraging open communication and reporting of potential risks is crucial for early identification and effective risk management.

8. Stress and Fatigue: Employee stress and fatigue can lead to lapses in judgment and increased likelihood of errors. Managing workloads and providing support can help reduce these risks.

9. Organizational Culture: The organizational culture and leadership tone set the tone for risk management practices. A culture that values risk management and accountability fosters effective risk mitigation.

10. Risk-Taking Behavior: The attitude toward risk-taking can influence how individuals and organizations approach risk management. Balancing risk and reward is essential for achieving strategic objectives.

11. Training and Capacity Building: Providing ongoing training and capacity building on risk

management topics ensures that employees are equipped to handle potential risks effectively.

12. Employee Engagement: Engaged employees are more likely to proactively identify and address potential risks. Fostering a culture of employee engagement can improve risk management outcomes.

13. Communication and Collaboration: Effective communication and collaboration among teams and departments help ensure that risks are addressed holistically and not overlooked.

14. Learning from Mistakes: Encouraging a learning culture that acknowledges and learns from past mistakes contributes to continuous improvement in risk management practices.

15. Human-Centric Approach: Recognizing the importance of the human factor in risk management and incorporating human-centric approaches in risk management strategies.

Understanding the human factor in risk management allows organizations to design risk management processes that consider human behavior, cognitive biases, and the impact of culture on risk perception. By leveraging the strengths and addressing the challenges of the human factor, organizations can enhance risk resilience and improve overall risk management effectiveness.

Training and Awareness

Training and awareness are essential components of effective risk management in organizations. They play a crucial role in empowering employees and stakeholders to identify, understand, and respond to potential risks. Here's how training and awareness contribute to successful risk management:

1. Risk Identification: Training employees to recognize and report potential risks enables early identification of uncertainties that could impact the organization.

2. Risk Understanding: Providing training on different types of risks and their potential consequences helps employees better understand the impact of risks on the organization's objectives.

3. Risk Appetite: Educating employees about the organization's risk appetite and tolerance helps align decision-making with the organization's risk management goals.

4. Risk Assessment: Training on risk assessment methodologies enables employees to evaluate the severity and likelihood of identified risks accurately.

5. Compliance and Regulations: Training on relevant laws, regulations, and industry standards helps ensure that employees are aware of compliance requirements and how to manage compliance-related risks.

6. Response Strategies: Educating employees about various risk response strategies, such as risk

avoidance, risk reduction, risk transfer, and risk acceptance, empowers them to contribute to effective risk mitigation.

7. Crisis Management: Conducting crisis management drills and simulations as part of training prepares employees to respond effectively during real crises.

8. Business Continuity: Training on business continuity planning helps employees understand their roles and responsibilities in maintaining critical operations during disruptions.

9. Cybersecurity Awareness: Raising awareness about cybersecurity risks and best practices helps employees protect sensitive information and prevent data breaches.

10. Reporting and Communication: Training employees on how to report risks and communicate incidents ensures that information flows effectively within the organization.

11. Risk Culture: Training and awareness initiatives contribute to building a risk-aware culture where employees understand the importance of risk management in achieving organizational objectives.

12. Stakeholder Engagement: Training stakeholders, such as suppliers and customers, about risk management practices fosters collaborative risk management across the value chain.

13. Continuous Improvement: Regular training sessions and awareness programs promote a continuous improvement mindset in risk management practices.

14. Senior Management Understanding: Training senior management on risk management concepts fosters their support and commitment to risk management initiatives.

15. Adaptability: Continuous training ensures that employees are equipped to handle emerging risks and changing risk landscapes.

Training and awareness should be an ongoing process to keep risk management practices up-to-date and aligned with organizational goals. It is essential to tailor training programs to different employee roles and levels of responsibility, ensuring that everyone understands their role in managing risks effectively. By investing in training and awareness initiatives, organizations can foster a risk-aware culture, enhance risk resilience, and achieve their strategic objectives more effectively.

Building a Risk-aware culture

Building a risk-aware culture is a fundamental aspect of effective risk management in organizations. A risk-aware culture encourages all employees to be vigilant about potential risks, take ownership of risk management, and actively contribute to identifying and mitigating uncertainties. Here are key steps to build a risk-aware culture:

1. Leadership Commitment: Leadership plays a crucial role in setting the tone for risk management. Senior executives and management should demonstrate a strong commitment to risk awareness and actively promote risk management practices throughout the organization.

2. Clearly Defined Risk Objectives: Clearly communicate the organization's risk management objectives and how they align with the overall business strategy. This helps employees understand the importance of risk management in achieving organizational goals.

3. Education and Training: Provide comprehensive training and education on risk management concepts, methodologies, and best practices. Ensure that all employees, from top to bottom, understand their roles in identifying and managing risks.

4. Open Communication: Foster a culture of open communication, where employees feel comfortable reporting potential risks and concerns. Encourage the sharing of risk-related information and lessons learned from past incidents.

5. Risk Ownership: Encourage employees to take ownership of risk management by empowering them to identify and assess risks related to their roles and responsibilities. This sense of ownership fosters a proactive approach to risk management.

6. Recognition and Rewards: Recognize and reward employees who actively contribute to risk identification, mitigation, and overall risk management efforts. Positive reinforcement reinforces the importance of risk awareness.

7. Integration with Decision-Making: Integrate risk management into decision-making processes at all levels of the organization. Encourage employees to consider potential risks when

making strategic, operational, and project-related decisions.

8. Continuous Improvement: Promote a culture of continuous improvement in risk management practices. Encourage employees to learn from past incidents and near-misses to enhance risk resilience.

9. Risk Reporting and Metrics: Establish clear risk reporting mechanisms and key risk indicators (KRIs) to monitor risk exposure and communicate risk information effectively.

10. Risk Tolerance and Appetite: Clearly define the organization's risk tolerance and risk appetite. This helps guide employees in making risk-informed decisions.

11. Training for Leadership: Provide training and awareness programs for leaders and decision-makers to strengthen their understanding of risk management concepts.

12. Role Modeling: Leaders and managers should lead by example and demonstrate risk-aware behaviors in their decision-making and actions.

13. Encourage Collaboration: Promote collaboration among different departments and teams in identifying and managing risks that may cut across organizational boundaries.

14. Adaptability: Encourage adaptability in risk management practices to address new and emerging risks.

15. Regular Review and Communication: Regularly review and communicate the organization's risk management strategy and outcomes to reinforce the importance of risk awareness and its impact on organizational success.

Building a risk-aware culture requires a concerted effort at all levels of the organization. By fostering a risk-aware culture, organizations can create a proactive and resilient environment that effectively addresses uncertainties and enhances overall performance.

Chapter 10

Case studies and lesson learned

Case studies and lessons learned in risk management provide valuable insights into real-world scenarios where risk management practices have succeeded or failed. Here are a few case studies and key lessons from each:

1. Case Study: Deepwater Horizon Oil Spill (2010)
Lesson Learned: The Deepwater Horizon oil spill was one of the largest environmental disasters in history. The incident highlighted the importance of effective risk assessment and management in high-risk industries. Lessons included the need for robust safety protocols, clear risk communication, and thorough emergency response plans to mitigate the impact of such catastrophic events.

2. Case Study: Target Data Breach (2013)
Lesson Learned: The Target data breach exposed the personal and financial data of millions of customers. This incident emphasized the

significance of cybersecurity and the need for strong data protection measures. Lessons included the importance of regular risk assessments, proactive monitoring of security systems, and swift response to potential breaches.

3. Case Study: Boeing 737 MAX Crashes (2018-2019)
Lesson Learned: The Boeing 737 MAX crashes highlighted the consequences of inadequate risk assessment and communication. The incidents underscored the importance of transparent risk communication and thorough risk analysis during the design and certification of complex systems.

4. Case Study: Lehman Brothers Collapse (2008)
Lesson Learned: The collapse of Lehman Brothers during the global financial crisis showcased the dangers of excessive risk-taking and lack of risk oversight. Lessons included the need for effective risk governance, stress testing, and risk diversification to prevent catastrophic failures.

5. Case Study: Fukushima Daiichi Nuclear Disaster (2011)

Lesson Learned: The Fukushima Daiichi nuclear disaster underscored the significance of disaster preparedness and resilience. The incident emphasized the importance of incorporating lessons from past accidents, emergency response planning, and effective risk communication in high-risk industries.

6. Case Study: Samsung Galaxy Note 7 Recall (2016)

Lesson Learned: The Samsung Galaxy Note 7 recall highlighted the importance of rigorous quality control and risk management in product development. The incident demonstrated the need for early identification of potential risks and swift action to address them to prevent significant financial and reputational damage.

7. Case Study: Tylenol Cyanide Poisoning Incident (1982)

Lesson Learned: The Tylenol cyanide poisoning incident resulted in the death of seven people and led to the tamper-resistant packaging standards. The case demonstrated the importance of crisis management, transparent communication, and responsible product safety measures.

These case studies offer valuable lessons on the importance of risk management in various industries and scenarios. They underscore the significance of risk identification, assessment, response planning, and communication in preventing or mitigating potential adverse outcomes. Organizations can learn from these cases to strengthen their risk management practices and enhance their ability to manage uncertainties effectively.

Real-life examples of effective risk management

Real-life examples of effective risk management showcase organizations that have successfully identified, assessed, and mitigated risks, leading to positive outcomes and minimizing potential adverse impacts. Here are a few notable examples:

1. Johnson & Johnson's Tylenol Recall Response (1982):

In 1982, Johnson & Johnson faced a crisis when several individuals died after consuming cyanide-laced Tylenol capsules. The company quickly recalled all Tylenol products from store shelves, cooperated with authorities, and kept the public informed through transparent and empathetic communication. Johnson & Johnson's decisive action and responsible handling of the crisis demonstrated effective risk management and helped rebuild consumer trust in the brand.

2. Google's Data Center Management:

Google has implemented effective risk management practices for its data centers to ensure uninterrupted service. They use predictive analytics to forecast potential equipment failures and proactively replace components before they cause service disruptions. By investing in redundancy and monitoring systems, Google has minimized the risk of data center outages, ensuring high availability of their services.

3. Walt Disney World's Hurricane Preparedness:
Walt Disney World in Florida is situated in a region prone to hurricanes. The park has a comprehensive hurricane preparedness plan in place, including protocols for guest and employee safety, securing property, and restoring operations post-hurricane. Disney's proactive approach to risk management has allowed them to efficiently handle severe weather events without compromising guest experience or safety.

4. NASA's Mars Rover Curiosity Mission (2012):
NASA's Mars Rover Curiosity mission involved high risks associated with landing a rover on the Martian surface. The project team performed extensive risk analysis, conducted simulations, and implemented contingency plans for potential challenges during the landing. The successful landing and ongoing success of the mission demonstrated NASA's effective risk management practices in space exploration.

5. Singapore Changi Airport's Runway Safety Program:

Singapore Changi Airport is renowned for its strong safety culture and effective risk management. The airport implemented a runway safety program that involved technological solutions, improved procedures, and regular safety training for airport personnel. As a result, the airport has maintained a strong safety record and minimized the risk of runway incidents.

6. Procter & Gamble's Supply Chain Risk Management:

Procter & Gamble (P&G) adopted a robust supply chain risk management strategy to anticipate and respond to potential disruptions. P&G closely collaborates with suppliers, uses advanced analytics for risk monitoring, and maintains strategic safety stock to minimize the impact of supply chain disruptions. This approach has helped P&G maintain continuity in product supply despite various global challenges.

These real-life examples demonstrate how effective risk management can lead to better outcomes, safeguarding an organization's reputation, profitability, and overall resilience. By learning from these successful practices, other organizations can strengthen their risk management capabilities and be better prepared to address uncertainties and challenges in their respective industries.

Avoiding common pitfall

Avoiding common pitfalls in risk management is essential to ensure the effectiveness of risk management practices. Here are some common pitfalls to watch out for and tips to avoid them:

1. Lack of Leadership Support: Lack of support from senior leadership can hinder the success of risk management initiatives. To avoid this, engage top management early on, demonstrate the value of risk management, and secure their commitment to allocate resources and promote a risk-aware culture.

2. Overlooking Emerging Risks: Failing to identify and address emerging risks can lead to unexpected disruptions. Regularly assess the risk

landscape, stay updated on industry trends, and conduct scenario analyzes to identify potential emerging risks.

3. Insufficient Risk Assessment: Inadequate risk assessment may result in underestimating or overlooking significant risks. Conduct thorough risk assessments using appropriate methodologies, involving subject matter experts, and considering historical data and external factors.

4. Siloed Risk Management: Isolating risk management in individual departments can lead to fragmented risk responses. Encourage collaboration and communication across departments to foster a holistic approach to risk management.

5. Complacency After Success: Relying solely on past successes may lead to complacency and overlook changing risk dynamics. Continuously reassess risk management strategies and adapt to evolving risk landscapes.

6. Ignoring Human Factor: Overlooking the human factor in risk management can lead to errors and failures. Provide comprehensive training, promote risk awareness, and involve employees at all levels in risk identification and mitigation.

7. Inadequate Risk Communication: Poor risk communication can hinder effective decision-making and response. Implement clear and timely risk communication protocols to ensure stakeholders are informed appropriately during incidents.

8. Lack of Contingency Planning: Failing to develop contingency plans can leave the organization vulnerable during crises. Create detailed contingency plans for various risk scenarios, outlining specific actions and responsibilities.

9. Over Reliance on Insurance: Relying solely on insurance without implementing risk mitigation measures can lead to underestimating risk

exposure. Insurance should complement risk management efforts, not substitute them.

10. Neglecting Lessons Learned: Failing to learn from past incidents can result in recurring mistakes. Conduct thorough post-incident reviews, identify lessons learned, and use them to improve risk management practices.

11. Unrealistic Risk Tolerance: Setting unrealistic risk tolerance levels may lead to excessive risk-taking or risk-averse behavior. Align risk tolerance with the organization's objectives and ensure it is communicated effectively.

12. Failing to Monitor Risk Indicators: Neglecting to monitor key risk indicators (KRIs) can result in missed warning signs. Establish a system to monitor KRIs and take timely action based on identified trends.

13. Lack of Regular Reviews: Failing to review risk management strategies regularly can result in outdated approaches. Schedule periodic reviews

and updates to ensure risk management practices remain relevant and effective.

By being mindful of these common pitfalls and implementing proactive risk management practices, organizations can enhance their resilience, protect their interests, and better navigate uncertainties in today's dynamic business environment.

Chapter 11

Future Trends in Risk Management

As the business landscape evolves, risk management practices continue to adapt to emerging challenges and opportunities. Here are some future trends in risk management:

1. Technology Integration: Risk management will increasingly leverage technology, including artificial intelligence, machine learning, and data analytics, to enhance risk identification, assessment, and monitoring. Automation will streamline risk reporting and enable real-time risk analysis.

2. Cybersecurity and Data Privacy: With the growing threat of cyberattacks and data breaches, organizations will prioritize cybersecurity and data privacy in their risk management strategies. The focus will be on securing sensitive data, implementing robust cybersecurity measures, and complying with data protection regulations.

3. Climate Change and ESG Risks: Climate change-related risks, environmental, social, and governance (ESG) factors will gain prominence in risk management. Organizations will assess the impact of climate-related events and ESG considerations on their operations, reputation, and financial performance.

4. Pandemic Preparedness: The COVID-19 pandemic has highlighted the need for robust pandemic preparedness plans. Risk management will place greater emphasis on ensuring business continuity, supply chain resilience, and crisis response in the face of future pandemics or health crises.

5. Supply Chain Resilience: Organizations will focus on building resilient supply chains to mitigate risks arising from disruptions, geopolitical tensions, and other global events. Supply chain diversification and agility will become crucial risk management strategies.

6. Regulatory Compliance: As regulations continue to evolve, risk management will place greater emphasis on staying compliant with changing laws and industry standards. Regulatory technology (RegTech) will play a significant role in automating compliance processes.

7. Geopolitical Risks: Organizations operating in a globalized world will address geopolitical risks arising from trade tensions, political instability, and changing international relations. Geopolitical risk analysis will be integrated into decision-making processes.

8. Integrated Risk Management: Integrated risk management (IRM) will become more prevalent, enabling organizations to manage risks across different categories (e.g., financial, operational, cyber) in a cohesive and holistic manner.

9. Emerging Risks and Scenario Analysis: Scenario analysis will be increasingly used to assess potential risks and opportunities arising from disruptive trends and emerging technologies.

Organizations will explore possible future scenarios to make risk-informed decisions.

10. Reputation Risk Management: With the impact of social media and instant communication, managing reputation risks will be critical. Organizations will prioritize building and safeguarding their reputations through effective risk communication and crisis response.

11. Supply Chain ESG Risks: In addition to resilience, supply chain risk management will incorporate ESG considerations, such as supplier sustainability and responsible sourcing practices.

12. Remote Work Risks: As remote work becomes more prevalent, risk management will address cybersecurity risks, data protection, and employee well-being in a virtual work environment.

Overall, the future of risk management will be characterized by adaptability, innovation, and a proactive approach to anticipate and address evolving risks. Organizations that embrace these trends and integrate risk management into their strategic decision-making will be better positioned to thrive in an increasingly uncertain world.

Technology and automation in risk Assessment
Technology and automation are revolutionizing risk assessments by enhancing efficiency, accuracy, and the ability to process large volumes of data. Here are some ways technology and automation are transforming risk assessments:

1. Data Analytics: Advanced data analytics tools and techniques enable organizations to analyze vast amounts of data to identify patterns, trends, and potential risks. This includes using machine learning algorithms to detect anomalies and predict emerging risks.

2. Real-time Risk Monitoring: Technology allows for real-time monitoring of key risk indicators (KRIs) and early warning signals. Automated alerts can notify risk managers about deviations from normal risk levels, enabling swift responses.

3. Predictive Risk Modeling: Technology enables the development of predictive risk models that use historical data and scenarios to assess the likelihood and impact of potential risks. This aids in proactive risk management and decision-making.

4. Risk Visualization: Data visualization tools help present complex risk data in a more accessible and understandable format. Dashboards and heat maps enable stakeholders to grasp risk insights quickly.

5. Artificial Intelligence (AI) in Risk Assessments: AI can analyze unstructured data from various sources, such as news articles and social media, to identify potential risks and sentiment trends that may impact the organization.

6. Risk Management Software: Dedicated risk management software automates various aspects of risk assessments, such as risk identification, assessment, and response planning. These tools streamline collaboration and reporting.

7. Cybersecurity Risk Assessments: Technology aids in conducting comprehensive cybersecurity risk assessments by scanning networks, identifying vulnerabilities, and assessing the effectiveness of security controls.

8. Remote Risk Assessments: Technology facilitates remote risk assessments, making it possible for risk professionals to assess risks across geographically dispersed locations efficiently.

9. Compliance and Regulatory Risk: Technology streamlines compliance risk assessments by automating data gathering, analyzing regulations, and ensuring timely compliance updates.

10. Scenario Analysis and Stress Testing: Technology supports complex scenario analysis and stress testing by running simulations to assess the impact of potential risks on the organization.

11. Risk Aggregation and Reporting: Automation helps consolidate risk data from different sources

and business units, enabling comprehensive risk reporting and analysis.

12. Continuous Monitoring: Technology enables continuous monitoring of risks, ensuring that risk assessments remain up-to-date and responsive to changing circumstances.

The integration of technology and automation in risk assessments empowers organizations to make data-driven decisions, enhance risk insights, and respond more effectively to potential uncertainties. However, it is essential to maintain a balance between technology and human judgment, as human expertise and critical thinking remain crucial in interpreting results and making risk-informed decisions.

Emerging risks and their impacts
Emerging risks are uncertainties that are currently evolving or have not been fully recognized, and they have the potential to significantly impact organizations and industries. The impact of emerging risks can be far-reaching, affecting

financial performance, reputation, operations, and strategic decision-making. Here are some examples of emerging risks and their potential impacts:

1. Cybersecurity Risks: With the increasing reliance on digital technologies and data, cyber threats are becoming more sophisticated. A cyber-attack can lead to data breaches, financial losses, reputational damage, and legal liabilities.

2. Climate Change and Environmental Risks: Climate change-related events, such as extreme weather events, rising sea levels, and natural disasters, pose risks to businesses and communities. Organizations may face disruptions in supply chains, property damage, and increased regulatory scrutiny.

3. Pandemic and Health Risks: The COVID-19 pandemic highlighted the potential impact of health risks on global economies and businesses. Pandemics and contagious diseases can lead to

widespread business disruptions, supply chain issues, and economic downturns.

4. Geopolitical Risks: Geopolitical tensions, trade disputes, and changes in international relations can affect global businesses. These risks can lead to supply chain disruptions, market volatility, and regulatory changes.

5. Technological Disruptions: Advancements in technology, such as artificial intelligence, automation, and blockchain, can disrupt industries and business models. Organizations may face challenges in adapting to new technologies or become obsolete if they fail to innovate.

6. Social and Demographic Changes: Changing societal norms and demographic shifts can impact consumer preferences and workforce dynamics. Organizations may need to adapt to changing customer demands and attract diverse talent.

7. Regulatory and Compliance Changes: Evolving regulations and compliance requirements can pose

challenges for businesses. Non-compliance may result in fines, reputational damage, and legal consequences.

8. Data Privacy and Ethics: Concerns about data privacy and ethical use of data can impact organizations' reputation and consumer trust. Organizations must navigate privacy regulations and ensure responsible data practices.

9. Supply Chain Vulnerabilities: Global supply chains face risks from geopolitical events, natural disasters, and demand fluctuations. Disruptions in the supply chain can lead to production delays and inventory shortages.

10. Financial Market Volatility: Market uncertainties and economic fluctuations can affect financial performance and investment decisions. Organizations may face challenges in managing financial risks and accessing capital.

Addressing emerging risks requires a proactive and agile approach to risk management.

Organizations must conduct regular risk assessments, scenario planning, and develop contingency plans to respond effectively to uncertainties. Staying informed about emerging trends, regulatory changes, and global developments is critical to identify and mitigate potential risks in a timely manner. Being prepared to adapt and innovate is essential for organizations to thrive in an increasingly dynamic and uncertain business environment.

Conclusion

Handling risk is a critical aspect of achieving organizational success and resilience in today's dynamic and uncertain business environment. It requires a proactive and systematic approach that involves identifying, assessing, and managing potential uncertainties. Here are key takeaways on how to handle risk effectively:

1. Risk Identification: Thoroughly identify potential risks that could impact the organization's objectives, operations, and stakeholders. Encourage employees at all levels to be vigilant in spotting and reporting risks.

2. Risk Assessment: Assess risks based on their likelihood and potential impact on the organization. Use data analytics, scenario analysis, and expert insights to understand the severity of risks.

3. Risk Management Plan: Develop a comprehensive risk management plan that outlines

strategies and response actions to address identified risks. Clearly define roles, responsibilities, and communication protocols during incidents.

4. Risk Mitigation Strategies: Implement appropriate risk mitigation strategies, such as avoiding, transferring, reducing, or accepting risks based on the organization's risk tolerance and objectives.

5. Technology and Automation: Embrace technology and automation in risk assessments and management to enhance efficiency, accuracy, and real-time monitoring.

6. Business Continuity: Establish a robust business continuity plan to ensure critical operations can continue during disruptions, such as natural disasters or crises.

7. Adaptability and Innovation: Stay agile and adaptable to address emerging risks and technological advancements. Encourage

innovation to explore new ways of managing risks effectively.

8. Communication and Stakeholder Involvement: Foster a culture of open communication and stakeholder involvement in risk management. Engage employees, suppliers, customers, and partners in risk awareness and response efforts.

9. Continuous Improvement: Continuously review and update risk management practices based on lessons learned from past incidents and changes in the risk landscape.

10. Compliance and Ethics: Prioritize compliance with laws, regulations, and ethical standards. Ethical behavior and responsible risk practices build trust and reputation.

11. Leadership Support: Gain strong leadership support and commitment to drive risk management initiatives across the organization.

12. Risk Awareness: Educate employees about risk management concepts and promote a risk-aware culture. Empower employees to contribute to risk identification and mitigation efforts.

By adopting a holistic and proactive approach to risk management, organizations can navigate uncertainties, seize opportunities, and build a resilient foundation for sustainable growth. Handling risk effectively requires continuous vigilance, adaptability, and collaboration among all stakeholders to safeguard the organization's interests and ensure long-term success.

In conclusion, effective risk management is a crucial discipline that organizations must embrace to navigate uncertainties, protect their interests, and achieve long-term success. It involves a systematic approach to identifying, assessing, and managing potential risks that could impact the organization's objectives, operations, and stakeholders.

To handle risk effectively, organizations should prioritize risk identification and assessment, leveraging technology and automation to enhance efficiency and accuracy. Developing a comprehensive risk management plan with clear response strategies is essential to mitigate identified risks. Emphasizing business continuity planning ensures critical operations can continue during disruptions, while fostering a risk-aware culture promotes proactive risk management at all levels.

Strong leadership support, stakeholder involvement, and open communication are vital in driving risk management initiatives and creating a risk-aware culture throughout the organization. Compliance with regulations and ethical standards builds trust and enhances reputation, while continuous improvement based on lessons learned fosters resilience in the face of evolving risks.

By being agile, adaptable, and innovative, organizations can respond effectively to emerging risks and embrace opportunities. Emphasizing risk management as an integral part of decision-making enables informed choices, while nurturing a proactive approach to risk handling ensures the organization's ability to thrive amidst uncertainty.

In conclusion, a well-structured risk management approach empowers organizations to seize opportunities, protect against potential pitfalls, and foster long-term sustainability in an ever-changing business landscape. Handling risk effectively is not merely a precautionary measure; it is a strategic imperative for organizations seeking to secure their future in an increasingly dynamic world.

Recap

Recap of the key concepts of handling risk:

1. Risk Identification: Thoroughly identify potential risks that could impact the organization's objectives, operations, and stakeholders. Encourage employees at all levels to be vigilant in spotting and reporting risks.

2. Risk Assessment: Assess risks based on their likelihood and potential impact on the organization. Use data analytics, scenario analysis, and expert insights to understand the severity of risks.

3. Risk Management Plan: Develop a comprehensive risk management plan that outlines strategies and response actions to address identified risks. Clearly define roles, responsibilities, and communication protocols during incidents.

4. Risk Mitigation Strategies: Implement appropriate risk mitigation strategies, such as avoiding, transferring, reducing, or accepting risks based on the organization's risk tolerance and objectives.

5. Technology and Automation: Embrace technology and automation in risk assessments and management to enhance efficiency, accuracy, and real-time monitoring.

6. Business Continuity: Establish a robust business continuity plan to ensure critical operations can continue during disruptions, such as natural disasters or crises.

7. Adaptability and Innovation: Stay agile and adaptable to address emerging risks and technological advancements. Encourage innovation to explore new ways of managing risks effectively.

8. Communication and Stakeholder Involvement: Foster a culture of open communication and stakeholder involvement in risk management. Engage employees, suppliers, customers, and partners in risk awareness and response efforts.

9. Continuous Improvement: Continuously review and update risk management practices based on lessons learned from past incidents and changes in the risk landscape.

10. Compliance and Ethics: Prioritize compliance with laws, regulations, and ethical standards. Ethical behavior and responsible risk practices build trust and reputation.

11. Leadership Support: Gain strong leadership support and commitment to drive risk management initiatives across the organization.

12. Risk Awareness: Educate employees about risk management concepts and promote a risk-aware culture. Empower employees to contribute to risk identification and mitigation efforts.

By incorporating these key concepts into their risk management practices, organizations can navigate uncertainties effectively, seize opportunities, and build a resilient foundation for sustainable growth. Handling risk successfully is not only a defensive strategy but also a strategic imperative for organizations looking to thrive in an ever-changing and dynamic business environment.

Encouragement to Implement Risk Management Practice

Implementing risk management practices is not just a prudent choice; it is a crucial step towards securing your organization's future and long-term success. Embracing risk management empowers you to navigate uncertainties with confidence, protect your interests, and seize opportunities for growth. Here's why you should encourage and prioritize risk management practices:

1. Enhancing Resilience: Risk management strengthens your organization's ability to withstand and recover from unexpected challenges. By identifying and mitigating potential risks, you can minimize disruptions and maintain business continuity even in times of crisis.

2. Seizing Opportunities: Risk management is not just about avoiding pitfalls; it also involves identifying and assessing opportunities. By understanding risks, you can make informed decisions to capitalize on favorable trends and industry shifts.

3. Safeguarding Reputation: Proactive risk management helps protect your organization's reputation and brand. By demonstrating responsible risk practices and crisis preparedness, you can build trust among stakeholders, customers, and investors.

4. Supporting Decision-Making: Incorporating risk analysis into your decision-making process enables you to weigh potential risks and rewards effectively. This risk-informed approach fosters strategic decision-making that aligns with your organization's objectives.

5. Boosting Stakeholder Confidence: Stakeholders, including investors, employees, and customers, seek assurance that you have a clear understanding of potential risks and are well-prepared to handle them. Effective risk management instills confidence in your organization's capabilities.

6. Complying with Regulations: Regulatory requirements are ever-evolving, and compliance is crucial to avoid legal and financial consequences. Risk management practices ensure that you meet compliance obligations and adapt to changing regulations.

7. Empowering Employees: Encouraging a risk-aware culture empowers employees at all levels to identify and report risks proactively. This collaborative approach harnesses the collective intelligence of your workforce.

8. Securing Long-Term Growth: Organizations that embrace risk management are better positioned to identify emerging trends and stay ahead of their competitors. Proactively managing risks leads to sustainable growth and a competitive advantage.

9. Driving Innovation: Effective risk management encourages innovation by providing a safe environment to explore new ideas and experiment with novel solutions. Taking calculated risks is

essential for progress and staying relevant in dynamic markets.

10. Demonstrating Leadership: Organizations that prioritize risk management demonstrate strong leadership and responsible governance. Such organizations attract investment, partnerships, and valuable talent.

In conclusion, implementing risk management practices is an investment in your organization's future. It fosters resilience, supports strategic decision-making, and boosts stakeholder confidence. Embrace risk management as a strategic imperative to navigate the complexities of today's business landscape successfully. Together, let's build a risk-aware culture that empowers your organization to thrive in an ever-changing world.

www.ingramcontent.com/pod-product-compliance
Lightning Source LLC
Chambersburg PA
CBHW072205290526
45794CB00004B/1660